CW00504380

UNDERCURRENTS

A Poetry Collection

YEMISI IBIDUNNI

Copyrighted Material

Copyright © 2017 Yemisi Ibidunni

All rights reserved

DEDICATION

My sincere thanks to all my family, friends and loved ones.
Special thanks to Femi, Elijah, Rotimi and Ann. Thank you
for the good times, support and inspiration.

"Water is the softest thing, yet it can penetrate mountains and earth. This shows clearly the principle of softness overcoming hardness."

— **Lao Tzu**

CONTENTS

STILL WATER

Still water

So calm and so blue.

Beautiful on the surface

Beautiful in its mysteries

How they wonder what lies beneath?

I am inviting and luring

Daring them to test my depths.

I do not rage like the stormy sea

Controlled and steady I stay instead.

I bury complex emotions

To take away hidden dangers.

You can walk beside my still waters

So calm and so blue.

I will bring you peace

Through the wells of my understanding,

I will quench your thirst

Through my overflowing love

But don't disturb my waters

So calm and so blue.

Don't mistaken my quietness

Or take for granted my passiveness,

For if you disturb my waters

You will be swallowed deep into my fortress.

So come,

Lay freely and honestly beside my still waters

So calm and so blue.

REJECTION

One by one, they walk.

I stare in a daze as they hurriedly wave goodbye

They were once my friends you know

But you see it's that time were they've got to go.

Hello somebody, then the door closes

Goodbye somebody.

Tick tock, tick tock,

Misery, misery, misery.

Another one gone

And that's how it goes,

They come and they go.

Yemisi's crazy, she makes no sense

Yemisi, KMT she's just a little girl.

"Hello mummy's little girl that yelps,

What a shame no one hears when you cry for help."

"Mummy mummy, am I alright?

He's touching me again, am I alright?"

"Shhhh mummy's little girl,

You doing just fine,

Touch me there,

Lick me here

You are doing just fine."

"Mummy mummy, am I alright?"

I don't think she wants to hear my cries

Yemisi's ugly, Yemisi smells

So the kids run fast,

Like they heard the school bell

Yank, they pulled her hair

Ouch there's glass in her leg

Tick tock, tick tock ,

Misery is looming

"No one likes you, you are so weird"

"You are a rat, haven't you heard"

"OMG, I thought you were my friend"

"No yemisi, you are just weird."

Tick tock, tick tock misery is looming

"I don't like you, leave me alone"

"But I love you"

"I said leave me alone."

So it starts to build,

Yemisi, you are ugly

Yemisi, you are weird,

Yemisi's smelly

Yemisi who cares?

So you don't have to tell me I'm ugly,

I'll show it to you.

You don't have to tell me to leave,

You'll leave real soon

You don't have to tell me I smell,

You'll smell my pain and my hurt

Then you'll run

Real fast, like them all...

CHINESE FLOOR

Like the Chinese floor

They do not see me.

Like the Chinese floor

I am worn out and weary.

Like the Chinese floor

They stamp on me.

Like the Chinese floor

I smell their feet.

Like the Chinese floor

I am nothing to them

But

Like the Chinese floor

I have a worth

Like the Chinese floor

I support them

Like the Chinese floor

I bear their weight

But

Soon I will break

Then they will see my worth

The worth of the Chinese floor.

Have you ever been rejected? I'm sure we all have in one way or another, it may have been small through a disapproving glance or huge like being bullied but we have all experienced that pain and embarrassment of being rejected. A terrible feeling of not being wanted, not feeling loved and not being accepted. Rejection is a part of life but if we do not know how to cope with it, it can be very damaging because it can lead to low self-esteem and self-rejection. For years, I felt rejected, not only by the outside world but by those closest to me, it broke me down, I was just a shell of the real me, I always doubted myself and felt bad about myself. I never stood up for myself; I was too concerned with other people's opinions instead of understanding and expressing how I felt, I wanted to please and through that I forgot to please me, to love me. It made me depressed, it made me hurt, it made me angry, I was mad like hell.

NO POWER OVER ME

I do not remember your face

Nor do I remember your name

I chose to let it go

Not dwell on what you robbed from me

So now you are just a faded memory

I took back my joy

You have no power over me

Not over my thoughts

Not over my body

Not over my soul

You are nothing

You could not break me

You are nothing

I am in control.

I was around seven years old when I was sexually molested. I do not remember a lot about it, just that I was meant to keep it a secret. I do not remember feeling that much fear. I didn't really understand what was going on, except that we were doing something not quite right. As I grew older, I started to understand what happened to me and from observing what was going on around me, I grew to distrust men. I had no one to run to, to discuss what had happened to me; you see I came from an African home and in my family, children were seen but not heard. I had no one asking me how I felt and I didn't feel safe enough to discuss what happened. I downplayed the abuse and didn't believe it had affected me but it was evident through the way I related with members of the opposite sex, I always wanted to please like the little girl who was asked to do something or another to prove I was a good girl. I was sexually vulnerable and open but I was never emotionally vulnerable. I put myself into an abusive pattern and didn't stop to think I deserved better, someone to care for my needs too. After a few failed relationships, I started to choose to love myself and start choosing men who were emotionally available and didn't want to waste my time. I decided to not put up with rubbish; I understood that I had been robbed of the perception of what a healthy sexual relationship should really be. I was hypersexualised and sex was a tool, a tool to please men and not myself. Now I know the value and sacredness of sex and how it's intertwine with what is going on with me spiritually and I am conscious about how I want to share my body. I learnt to be open about what happened yet not dwell on it. I accept it happened but I refuse to let it define me. I refuse to let it rob me of my joy; I refused to let it break me, I became conscious of the decisions I was making and didn't let what happened define my destiny.

WHAT DO YOU SEE?

When you look into my eyes, what do you see?

Can you see me drowning or

Can you see me smiling?

Can you see I'm hurting and

On the verge of dying?

I'm sure you can see nothing

Because I am so empty

Tell me you will rescue me

From all my hurt and my pain

Tell me you will love me

Tell me you will care,

Hold me in your arms and I plead

Don't leave me here

Show me how to live

Show me how to smile

I need you to show me how

If not, I'll drown and die

Treat me like a baby

Treat me fresh and new

Feed me tenderly with love

And make my heart so full

Give me what I need

Give me what I want

You have to do something

Before I rot to nothing

I'm calling

I'm shouting

I'm pleading

Just look into my eyes

And see me crying

If you stop looking

I'm sure I'll drown and die.

LONELINESS

It's me and loneliness lying in the dark tonight

Tears roll down my eyes, as I turn left and right

Wondering why they whisper so many lies,

Wondering why they even bother to try.

Why don't they stay the hell away from me?

When their intention is to come my way then hide

Why do they pretend to care?

 To pick me up then drop me back here?

What is the point of writing when they still won't hear?

They told me they loved me, so why am I so lonely?

They told me they loved me so why the f*** am I lonely tonight?

Crying again with loneliness tonight?

TIRED OF BEING TIRED

I am so sick and tired

I feel so restless

I feel I've reached the height of my destination.

I have had enough.

I can't bear it any longer.

I'm tired of this constant pain

Tired of my insecurities

Tired of feeling worthless

Tired of judging eyes

Tired of my efforts that goes unnoticed

Tired of the tears I shed at night.

I'm tired of the brave face I have to put up

I'm tired of the hell I call earth

I'm tired of the injustice in this cruel cold world

I'm tired cos I feel lost and confused

I'm tired of drowning in my sorrows.

Father above, have mercy on me

And hear my call

For I am truly tired of it all

All I want is to be happy and content

Most of all, I'm tired of being tired.

FRUSTRATION

I stare at the t.v

I stare beyond the t.v

I stare over the t.v

I stare till I see no more.

My eyes goes blank

My mind travels far

How did I get here?

No ambition, no care

Well, no care over what I used to value first

And there is the stillness,

The feeling of going no where

Scared that I will make no progress

So I try to erase the fear

And focus on my reality, which I share

With my beautiful baby boy for whom I care

And though my world is less than perfect

And I am so confused about what's next,

I'll hold my head up with each and every step

And I'll use this opportunity to grow

In areas to me unknown

And I'll believe that something greater is near

And though it is not here yet

I am grateful for each and every breathe

Knowing my God will never give me more than I can bear.

Am I better than her?

Is she prettier than me?

Maybe if I was thinner

Maybe if I was thicker

Maybe if I was fairer

Or if the tone of my skin was better

Deep are my insecurities, they eat away at me.

Maybe if I was smarter

Maybe if I was taller

Maybe I should have said that

Maybe I shouldn't wear this

Deep are my insecurities, they eat away at me.

Does she really like me?

Does he really like me?

Why is she so quiet?

Why didn't he call?

Deep are my insecurities, they eat away at me

Maybe I'm not good enough

Maybe I don't belong

Maybe....

Maybe.....

They eat away at me.

I get depressed from time to time. You see depression is different from that empty void that humans feel when they realise nothing will make them complete; that emptiness might lead to depression. Some people try to 'complete themselves' or make themselves happy by filling their time up with work or hobbies, keeping themselves busy, their minds busy, not meditating; they plough through lives maybe not contemplating what is going on within or around them, till one day, they are forced to be still and realise that nothing can make them complete or constantly happy then they crash and become depressed. That was me at the age of 25, broken. I had spent my life on the fast lane, ticking off boxes, conquering, moving on to the next, believing I was in control. Self-reflection, what is that? Meditation, whose got the time? Then time stood still, I was forced to think, to look within, I had all the time in the world. I was a single mum of a young boy of three. I had just dropped out of a masters course, I had just experienced a traumatic separation from my ex and I had just settled into a place, couldn't call it home yet. During facing the pressures of being homeless, finding a new home, moving from place to place, decorating a place to make it liveable and amongst this trying to ensure that my little boy was ok; I had no time to think, not before, but now, I could clearly see the destruction I had created and one day I broke down. It must have happened within the course of 3 days but I deteriorated till my mind was faded. I was erratic, I locked my little boy and I in a room convinced I was keeping us away from harm, you see I remember everything clear as day but back then, my mind was a confused mess. Luckily a friend came to see me that day, I argued with her and she knew I was behaving erratically so she called my mum and my brother, who then called the ambulance. I was taken to the psych ward, they gave me some pills to sleep and I was better the next day. How did I get there? I still don't know. I still fear that I might return there but what did I learn? I learnt to be mindful and accept that nothing but God can fill that empty void. I started to understand what was going on within, to reflect and meditate on what I was feeling and confront and battle it with constant reminders of God's word and love for myself and for my situation before it overwhelms me. So now I no longer get depressed over that, however depression is triggered when I have a lack of energy; I start to resist the flow of life and the gates of the dark muddy waters of my mind pours in, gush after gush, it weighs heavy on my mind and I get stuck in the darkness unable to fight it because my body and my mind is tired. I dwell on my time constraints, energy constraints, financial constraints, wanting to do stuff that sometimes time doesn't permit, or I have no energy to do or I have no money to do, thinking the world is having more 'fun' than me, I think of the things I haven't accomplished yet but I pick myself up after a second, after an hour, after a day, depending on the strength of my mind, I renew my mind, I remember God's word, he has plans of good for me, he shall never forsake me, I will be okay.

I will never know your pain

My dear

I will never know your pain.

If only I can take it away

I try not to cry

But my tears won't stop

Knowing the greatness of your loss.

You are so strong

My dear

It hurts too much.

I will never know your pain.

SECRET

They are mine

They make me feel safe.

Leave me alone,

I am not telling

They are mine.

I am not sharing,

They are mine.

Go away, it scares me

Come closer, please don't judge me.

It engulfs me,

Its darkness surrounds me.

Release me

Comfortable darkness

Release me;

But you make me feel safe

You are mine.

You make me feel safe

You are mine.

Sometimes I want to hurt you

At times it's so bad

I want to kill you

And yet, I say 'I love you.'

I ask myself how can I love and hate

I think of your smile

I think of your touch

I think of your strength

I love you

Then...

I think of what you said

And how you treat me like dirt

I can say 'I hate you'

Why do you hate me?

Why don't I please you?

Why do you reject me

And make me feel a fool?

Do you know it brings me down?

Do you know it makes me cry?

Do you know it cuts my heart

So it bleeds every single night?

I want to yell out 'I love you,

Why don't you love me back?'

I need to run away

But still, I want to stay

I'm waiting to hear you love me, to take me as I am

I have been battered

With so many words

I have been battered

Till I feel no more.

I'm tired

I'm cold

I feel so empty

Beside you all

I want to hate you

But I can't

I want to hate you

But I don't

Why don't you love me, I'll never know

I look in the mirror and I swear I'm beautiful

Inside and out, I know I'm beautiful.

You either love a person or not they say; but it is always important to consider whether pursuing a relationship with a person you have fallen in love with is worth it, however, sometimes you are already in the relationship when you figure out that this is not the right person for you. What do you do then? Do you carry on in fear, afraid of moving on; dwelling on the wasted years or do you cut your losses, see it as a lesson learnt and keep on living. There are many reasons why pursuing a relationship with someone you love may not be worth the hassle that it may bring such as wrong timing, different life values, the other person being emotionally unavailable but for those who have been through the heartache, you can say that looking at the experience in a different light, you have learnt and gained something. Sometimes we must go through these experiences that chew us up and spit us in order to be re-born and be on a higher plane. For me, I fell in love at a tender age of 15 and I wish someone had told me then that you can love someone but not necessary be with them, oh well, I probably wouldn't have listened, always been the type to find things out myself and anyways it was just part of my lessons in life. We were young, we were incompatible, we were strong headed, must I say a bad recipe for a fulfilling relationship but yet we were at it for many years, only mainly because I was holding on, fighting for something that was a lost cause, too unsure of myself and didn't love myself enough to move on from the hurt. I went on to love other people before I learnt this very lesson that you can find love in a hopeless place.

INFATUATION

Baby, I know you are not meant for me

But you have me so weak at the knees

The look in your eyes

Have got me hypnotised

No other man got me feeling like this.

I'll never forget our very first kiss,

The feel of your lips had me going on a trip

But I'm trying real hard to get a grip

No other man got me feeling like this.

You got me calling your name

Feigning for you

Waiting on you

But you'll never know

Cos I'll always be keeping my cool.

OMG, you are back again

My knight in shining armour to save the day,

Oh how happy I am, I can't complain

Of how you suddenly left the other day

I want to ask, 'will you stay?

How long for? Please give a date?'

So I can brace myself against the pain

Of when you run off into the night again;

I want to hug you but I'm afraid that I won't let go and

I can't bear the shame of letting you know that

I'm never the same when you go

And I pray, oh yes I prayed,

For the day that your way will be my way,

So we can walk this road every day,

And leave my sorrows far at bay.

For you and I are special, like diamonds in the sky

You make me come alive, oh you get me so high

So please think twice before you leave me

Feeling high and dry.

MR RIGHT NOW

He's doing the right things

Saying the right words

Touching the right places

Hitting the right spot

But I have been here before

Walked this road and sailed similar oceans

Bought this T-shirt in small

And I ain't about to wear it no more.

He will talk real nice

Insist that you are his trophy price

But within a throw of a dice

His true colours will shine

He'll be eyeing your friends

And he'll no longer be answering your calls

You'll hear his phone conversations

And realise he talks real nice to them all.

I ain't trippin though

Fool me once, shame on you

Fool me twice, then I'm the fool

But I won't be a fool for you.

So go on and do the right thing

It makes me feel you care

Go on and say the right words

It's music in my ears

Go on and touch the right places

Its making me real wet

Go on and hit the right spot,

It's making me scream oo yeah

But that's all it is

And for now, that's all you are

The man doing the 'right thing',

But it takes a lot more than that

For you to be the man who wins my heart.

You said that you would not settle for less

Assuming I would not have abandoned the rest

Not knowing that I would have put you first

Cos it pumps strongest for you, that organ beneath my left breast.

Why couldn't you see I cared?

Or where you blinded by unfounded fears?

You may have thought it made no sense

How I could move easily to other affairs

But you never made it clear how much you felt

And I waited and waited till my feelings could not contain itself

And even when those feelings were expressed,

It was never fully reciprocated until there was a posed threat,

Only then, did you make a step and I believed we were on our way there;

But I lost you altogether again

We couldn't get past the storm

And it rained like it will never stop.

Boy, you shouldn't have doubted my feelings were strong;

But you did and now we are back to square one.

WHAT DO I HAVE TO DO?

Would you love me more if you saw me

Breakdown and cry,

Begging the universe to make us right?

Would you love me more if you saw

How I cling to the thought of you and I?

Would you love me more if you knew how much I hurt

When you dismiss and ignore my calls?

Would you love me more if you could feel my pain

Knowing we are making it rain?

I want you to know that I am not as independent as I seem

Finding my soul mate is also my dream.

I want you to know that I want to understand you

Only so that I can be right for you,

Even knowing with gloom that the zodiac

Predicts our relationship doomed.

They say true love prevails,

I want to believe so

Yet I lay here all lost and confused

Cos I tried so hard to make it work

To someone somewhat similar to you

And see where that got me,

Feeling drained and misused.

So baby, I'm scared, so scared to love you

And yet I'm torn, cos my heart points only to you

Tell me I am wrong and that you and I are right

Tell me I am wrong and that we will be alright

Hold me tight, please let's stop the fights

Please help me understand you

Please understand me too,

So I can open my heart to you

And feel yours too.

MR GEMINI

Well baby, I think I have thought this through.

The question is 'Will I always be your number 2',

Always competing like the twin in you?

Will I ever grasp your heart,

Or will the quest for it tear me apart?

Must I always dance this tune with you,

Sway my hips and be your fool?

Must I always tease you out of that hole,

That one you run to when the intensity of my love shows?

Run into my arms, I hear you say

But will you be there, will you stay?

You capture me with your charm and intelligence

And yet you bother me with your nonchalance and negligence

So let me know, Mr Gemini, will you be there,

Steady and strong, showing you care?

Or will you forever blow,

Like your sign air?

Cos if that is so,

Then goodbye my dear.

Love, oh boy! That word love, used so frequently and so recklessly; not taking into account the power of those 4 letters. The action of that word, I believe, can conquer anything and unite us all. You see it amazes me when two people stop dating, they turn cruel to one another, I'm like 'were you only being nice because you were attracted to one another?', further more I'm baffled by those relationships where someone utters the words 'I love you' but are just downright mean and abusive, leaving the other person feeling confused and lost; like Mary j Blige says 'this ain't love.' I have had to learn the hard way what true love really means and I believe that as individuals, we have to learn to be conscious about love because love is a conscious act. I have already established that there are reasons why two people who love each other shouldn't get into a relationship but sometimes we enter into relationships with people who do not love us. You see loving someone is hard work because it sometimes goes against our egoistic wishes but because you love them you make the effort, you make the sacrifice. It is not easy to forgive, it is not easy to be patient, it is not easy to trust, it is not easy to face your demons and it is not easy to be vulnerable and honest. Like I explained earlier things were not great between my ex and I but I believe that if there was true love we could have got through it, yes we were young and incompatible to some degree but haven't you heard or met couples whose relationships worked even though they were young and incompatible; of course you have. They worked through it, they made some sacrifices, they made compromises, and they accepted their flaws. There are so many ways in which people define love, to me, love is not a fairy-tale; it encompasses the light and darkness of humans, it is painful yet joyful, it is tragic yet beautiful; be careful and diligent with your

46

love, hold it in the highest regard because it is easy for the little cracks of lies, secrets and harsh words to break a building; we are humans not pillars of stone, actions have repercussions and there is only so much one can take. You do not need too much water under your bridge of love. Love has a lot of ingredients, you can't just say it; you must act upon it and you must give it your all.

You say you can love two people at once

I somewhat agree you can

But you see that feeling you call love

I call it something else

I call it attraction

I call it passion

I call it understanding

I call it rapport

I call it a feeling of harmony where you feel support

But you see this thing called love

It requires much more

It requires honesty

It requires empathy

It requires compassion

It requires compromise

It requires a sort of pain and suffering

That comes from the wisdom of self-sacrifice

For you see this kind of love can never be disguised

And it takes so much effort

To provide this kind of comfort

That you better make sure

That the person in question

Is someone that brings you sufficient pleasure

In compromising yourself, then

You can both surrender and submit

To the power of this thing called love

And any problems you encounter

Will surely be conquered

Because you will both be fighting

As a solid united one.

The way he loves me.

Oh, just look at the way he loves me

I just love the way he loves me

I can't complain for he does not miss a thing

Tell me, is this what true love is?

Cos I feel understood, I feel at peace

And finally I can be the real me

No longer worrying about how to please

He loves and accepts the whole me

He sees it differently but tells me as it is

I'm free to express my views just like him

And we are determined to create a solid team

And for me, I want nothing more than this

For I can speak my truth with total ease

Yet compromise if we disagree

He helps me be a better me

And though some has said that

This kind of love lacks chemistry,

I have never felt more motivated

To love my king

In every single way,

I love my King.

I say 'I love you'

You respond you love me too

But what does this mean?

Would you stand by me through all my flaws?

Holding me up in times when I fall?

Hearing me out when I call?

Would you love me even when you dislike me?

Even when you despise my ways,

When I irritate you to your very core?

I do not blame you if you cannot

Because what I ask is extremely tough

And if not for the grace of God,

An impossible task for us all.

For we are only human and our flesh so weak

Prone to temptation

And slave to illusions.

So I look to my saviour, my creator, my provider

For all that I need,

For you alone cannot give it to me,

And I believe,

And I decree,

That my Jesus is more than enough for me.

His love makes me glow

In him, I grow

Through him, my blessings flow

I decree,

He is more than enough for me.

CAN I TRUST YOU?

In the presence of your love, I get so confused

Always need to be reassured

In order to feel secure

Baby I need your attention,

I need your devotion

I need your patience

For times when things get tense

Please do not come to the conclusion

That I am weak, needy and insecure

Cos I am far from that

But my feelings for you makes

Me want to show you the deepest writings in my heart

I don't want to hide it

But I'm scared you might run from it

So sometimes I put on a brave front

Acting tough with a humorous force

But internally I am soft

Just need your love cos I am ready to give mine

Don't want to hurt you

Just want to be there for you

I can't help it but

I'm just trying to play cool

Trying to not be your fool

Don't want to play no games,

Do you understand me?

Can I trust you?

VALENTINE

He whispered, 'would you be my valentine?'

I smiled and replied 'would you always be mine?'

He looked confused and somewhat puzzled

So I say,

Do you.... **V**olunteer your heart to me;

Avail yourself to....

Lend your help in times of need?

Extend your hand when I'm trouble deep

Never turn your back, this promise you shall keep.

Time will tell how serious you maybe

Integrity, a character I seek

Noble and nice, nurturing and kind

Eternally and forever mine.

He smiled and replied 'yes, now be my valentine.'

TWO BECOMES ONE

She was a seed, he was her water

She was his water, he was a seed.

They laid on a love so fertile

A love that provided all they need.

God was their sunshine, he shone from high above

They slowly grew and together they blossomed.

What do I see? I see devotion

What do I see? I see the truth

And how do I know?

From the way it makes me feel

And how do I feel?

I feel hope cos I see a love where one can grow

And nothing more beautiful for in their development it shows.

She is a better woman

And he is a better man

She cares for his needs; in the same way

He provides and shields her by his deeds

They are solid

They are united

They are family

Two became one.

I want it all

Give me everything

No stone left unturned.

All of your mind

I want to understand it

All of your body

I want to memorise it.

All of your soul

I want to intertwine mine to it.

I am your woman

I want it all.

All of your dirty thoughts

I will re-enact

All of your wounds

I will heal

All of your secrets

I will keep

I am your woman

I want it all.

All of your habits

I will study

All of your unchangeable flaws

I will accept

All of your needs

I will fulfil

I am your woman

I want it all

All of your dreams

I shall cherish

All of your values

I shall uphold

All of you

I shall honour

I am your woman

I am your vessel

Fill me.

I want it all.

It is all yours.

You better take it.

You better make me feel like your woman

You better bring it.

No need to ask permission

I'm always ready.

Don't hold back

I'll match your rhythm

Wherever

Whenever

I'm always willing

Whatever way you like it

I said

You better make me feel like your woman.

Dear husband

Come find comfort between my soft ample breasts

Come find peace

Whilst I caress your strong chest

Come find paradise

In between my rounded thighs

Come find desire

As you fill my flesh

And whisper you're mine.

I think human beings are funny, the way people can be so self-righteous, thinking they are better than another or that their way of thinking is right. Have you ever heard of the saying "what you see in others exist in you" or "You can't see yourself clearly till you see yourself through the eyes of others", we need to adopt this way of thinking to be open and tolerant with others, we are designed naturally to make judgements, to put people in boxes; it organises our thinking, it makes things easier to see but as we know some things are not black and white. People's lives and people's realities are based on their perception, so who are we to judge; we should all try to understand and learn a thing or two; I once heard that true wisdom is the ability to view something from different point of views. We are all the same but different.

MIRROR

Looking at you, looking at me

It's clear how very different we are

With different coloured hair

And different coloured eyes

You would think you will struggle to

Figure out how you resemble I,

But take a look very closely

And you'll get your answers quite quickly.

Capable of making each other smile, this we both share

The ability to not care,

The potential to lash out in anger and

The possibility of controlling our temper;

Insincerity we could all show

Integrity, a word we all know

So next time you are about to judge another fellow

Or consider them your number one foe,

Remember you can also display similar actions

Or fall in the same footpath tomorrow

For humans we are;

But free will we have and

The choice will always remain ours

To love others and be slow to anger;

For deeply I perceive,

How similar we may be,

Therefore we all need to be

Ready and quick to forgive.

FAR FROM PERFECT

Now I'm back, stronger than ever

Better than stronger

Confident and more,

And though it's true

Many of my friends have gone astray

They were never really here to stay

They were my experiences, my price to pay

For the lessons I had to learn along the way

And I'd like to thank those people for the pain

Cos I am a better person for it today

Please don't get me wrong, they were not entirely to blame

Deep were my insecurities, I could not communicate

But now I'm grateful for every experience

Though it may hurt after long drawn out ends

But I understand and I am aware,

That we are humans, and far from perfect

So I will try and I will amend

My impatient ways if you also accept

That you make mistakes and are not

Willing to contend or show pretence

So we can apologise, move on and

Appreciate every moment that we have left.

Who am I? Why am I here? How did I get here? What is my purpose? What is it all about? Sounds familiar? I have asked myself these questions so many times and I have engaged in conversations with people about this very topic, people wondering why they were put on this earth; you know what strikes me; everyone is looking for something big. They want to be famous, known or respected as this provides some kind of validation of their existence; they want to be 'somebody' like they are not yet 'somebody', and you know what, I do not blame them because we have been brain-washed and conditioned from our very beginning to think that unless we are known to the world, up there in society and living like the joneses', we are not worth the ground we stand on so we see people run themselves to the ground striving to accomplish what their hearts are not set on just to receive validation for their existence. Ask yourself, 'why am I doing this?', 'in whose eyes am I successful?' because as Maya Angelou once said "success is liking yourself, liking what you do and liking how you do it." You know what I say to those people wondering what their existence is about, I tell them "your existence is enough, your heart is enough and your dreams are enough, because everything changes because you are here". You see, as long as you are being who you are, being what God designed you to be and following your heart, you are fulfilling your purpose here on this earth. Did you ask to be born? No; yet here we are in a hurdled mass in earth. Now let's think of ourselves as a scientific matter, an atom (let's take hydrogen (H) for example) and our family and friends as a molecule ($H2O$); when an atom is added to another atom, there is a change in dynamic, a change in structure, meaning whenever 'you' as an existing person is added to an existence, there is an immediate change.

Every atom can produce atomic energy when there is a change in its sub-atomic mass (protons and nucleus), now think of your spirit, your inner being as the protons/nucleus; when something happens to stir your spirit, so for example someone made you happy or someone made you mad, you emit an energy because an energy has been transferred to you and as we all know energy is transferred not destroyed; so wherever you go with that energy, it is transferred onto something else causing a change in something, meaning your energy causes a change in your environment and it affects the people around you. We also know that energy can be changed by different forces meaning depending on what force is driving you as a person, your energy can be changed from positive to negative, negative to positive, for example somebody makes you feel jealous(energy) because they have a car you desire but you take that energy and channel it towards bettering yourself('new' energy) by aiming to get the car for yourself; and the 'new' energy can be transferred on; so for example somebody gets inspired by your efforts in getting the car of your dreams and does the same for themselves....Phew! So I know I have been on a long rant about how we change our environment and eventually the world through a small way but I hope you can see that by just being yourself you change those around you, have you heard of the saying 'be the change you want to see in the world' or 'your existence is evidence that this generation needs something that your life contains', it is so true. Be who you are, not what your parents or teachers said you will be, not what the world said you should be but who you want to be without fear. Your existence is enough.

As I sit here contemplating my existence

I ponder the question, 'who am I?'

I would like to tell you, I am beautiful

But I have done some ugly things.

I would like to tell you I am smart

But trust me, I can be quite daft.

I would like to tell you I'm funny

But my eyes don't always shine bright with laughter.

I would like to tell you, I am social, so

Tell me why do I feel so alone?

Then I look to define my existence through my plenty roles

I tell you, I am a mother

Full of nurture and care;

I tell you, I am a mother

Filled with guilt and fear.

Then I remember, I am also a friend

Who will always be there.

I tell you, I am a friend

Then I recall their calls that I sometimes neglect.

I tell you, I am a wife

Submissive to my head

I tell you, I am a wife

Filled with sorrows and tears.

I am a bunch of contradictions; I do not fit a box

My thoughts clouds in frustration to solve this very question

Who am I? It breeds confusion

Who am I? I am my choices good and bad

Who am I? The light bulb clicks

Who am I? I just am.

YOLO, you only live once

So what are you gonna do with your life?

The question is what is life?

A person defines life

Life in itself is an entity,

A space waiting to be filled

Life in itself is just a quality

That differentiates us from the dead

Life in itself has no meaning

It is up to us to create that meaning

Life's only certain destination is death

The rest is up to us to decide

Don't waste your life searching for its meaning,

It has none,

Instead open your hearts and be true to yourself

Fill your life with what is real to you.

Remember every experience, good or bad

Is an experience.

Live it, learn from it, remember or forget it but do not regret it.

Regret only brings tears and please do not fear,

It only limits your personal sphere.

Your life is like a mouth waiting to be fed

Feed it but feed it wisely

Be careful what you put in your mouth

Remember not everything sweet is good for you

And not everything sour will make you puke.

A trim waistline is not achieved by eating everything the mouth wants,

It is achieved by self-control and by sacrificing some wants.

In the same way, living according to your wants will not result in a fulfilled life

Don't let another hand feed your stomach because that hand feeds it with what tastes good to them,

Making it their life.

Life is not a dress rehearsal, once you eat, you cannot take back the food.

If you eat something bad, if it hurts, you'll always remember.

A fulfilled life is brought about by those moments were we show compassion and integrity

Because when the end comes, we measure the significance of our lives

Not by how much we have achieved

But by how much we have valued and loved others

Ultimately, to live is to have loved.

YOLO, you only live once.

FAITH

Like the Children of the sky,

I fly,

My wings are light,

Free from worry,

I twist and turn in delight.

My faith takes me higher

And against the beautiful colours of sunrise,

I break into a joyful dance,

Swooshing and Fluttering

Without a care of today or tomorrow,

I sing beautifully

I laugh hysterically.

I am okay.

I will be okay.

Today

Tomorrow

And

Always.

When I feel fear
I close my eyes
Picture my head on you
I feel your warm embrace.

When I cry out in distress
I close my eyes
Picture my head on you
You wipe the tears from my face.

When stuck in the darkest corners of my mind
I close my eyes
You whisper your holy words
You lift me out into the light.

When heavily burdened with the pressures of life.
I close my eyes
I let go and picture myself fall into your loving kindness.
Heavenly Father
You are with me.

I look down at you;

As your head nuzzles my breasts,

I am speechless,

Dumbfounded,

Silenced by your awesomeness.

I close my eyes,

My head tilts towards the direction of the sky

I whisper

Thank you.

MY BEAUTIFUL BLACK BOYS

My boys

My beautiful boys

My beautiful black boys

How do I protect thee?

My precious gems

How do I shield thee?

My future and my heirs

How do I guide thee?

In a world so bleak

My mind ceases to ease

How do I raise thee to be bold black men?

With the issues that plague our race

And in the mindlessness of our world today,

I ask myself if I have made a mistake

In bringing you into a world that cannot differentiate your face

And with a heart riddled with guilt and fear,

I get on my knees and I

Pray, pray, pray.

NOT EASY

Bored to death

Tired as heck

Moved to tears

It's not always easy

Being a mum.

Motherhood, the toughest task I know. Where to begin? Is it the self-sacrifice; giving them the energy and time they need when all you want is sleep, have 'me time' or get some privacy but yet again you have to stay up singing a rhyme song to put them to sleep? Or is it your baby chewing on your nipple all night or reminding your child for the umpteenth time to put their shoes in the right place? Is it the fear and anxiety that eats you up daily, wondering if they will be okay whatever age they are? When they are a baby, you are a human scanner/ detector looking for objects that they might ingest, then you pray for when they are older, more independent, then you remember the fear that comes with that, drugs, bullying, accidents, death, kidnapping, unprotected sex, irresponsible choices. Or is it the guilt of when you overreacted, or of how you made them watch too much T.V or how they heard you fighting with your partner or the long hours you are working, wondering the whole time 'what damage am I causing?' Or is it the daily mundane routine, cleaning, washing up, laundry never ending? A spotless house is a distance dream; if you manage to put on a dress or jeans, that's a good day especially when your kids are so little. Or is it when one of the questions that pop into your head first thing you wake up is 'what's for dinner?' So I worry and I ponder being me, being a mum, feeling the lack of energy, the restraints, I'm on a hamster wheel but amongst the chaos, the pain, the stress, I try to focus on the joy and when the opportunity presents itself, I take a break from being a mum and just do me. This is not a complaint just stating my truth, the truth of motherhood; but like everything in life, anything worth having is hard work!!! So to the mummies out there doing the best you can, I respect you. To the mummies feeling a little down from the stress and hard work, I empathise with you, to the single mother, the step mother, the working mother, the stay at home mothers, you are doing a great job; take each day as it comes, do your best and try not to worry about the rest; please let's not judge each other; you constantly see mums trying to outdo one another or read articles of one type of Mum putting down the choices of another Mum, let's stop the labelling, the judging, the pressures; we are all in this together so we should try to be supportive of one another regardless of the choices one makes to parent. Lastly to the ladies who have been told they will never conceive or are struggling and really want a baby, I will never know your pain, I will never walk in your shoes but know that I say take heart, don't lose hope, stay strong, I'm sorry your choice was taken from you but don't believe the lies your mind whispers in your dark times. You have a lot to give and a lot of good to birth into the world.

DESTRUCTION

Never walk about in life thinking you know it all

Cos I can only guarantee that you will fall

Only God grants real wisdom,

Which will be the key to his kingdom

Do not be ignorant, do not be dumb but

Be these things and you shall be destroyed at your own call.

Don't be fooled to think that you have got somebody

Cos truth be told, you ain't got anybody

You are here alone, you will fight alone

Friends will come, friends will go

Some might stay, but till what day?

'We are family' we all say

But wasn't it your family that made you cry the other day

Hark; remember to whom we all pray

When we feel we've gone astray

Oh yes, he is the one that will be with you all the way

When you are troubled, alone and feeling betrayed.

Ladies, Ladies, Ladies

Please can I talk to you?

For I know you've been hurting lately

Ain't got a clue on what to do

They told you to be a good woman

Submissive and loyal,

They told you to be a good woman

See now where has that got you?

You are filled with rage, filled with pain

Deep cut bruises

Bitterness running through your veins

Eyes sunken in with sorrow

Tears pour out beyond tomorrow

Trying to cleanse your soul

But the hurt is taking its toll and

Round and round we go.

Hatred is replacing the old

They better watch out now, you've got no remorse to show

You are going to pull them down, your madness, they'll get to know

You chain your heart, they can't reach you now

You think you are safe till you realise even you can't reach your heart's gate

You locked you out, you are imprisoned, trapped, looking in from afar

Who have you become now?

During the war, you lost your soul, created a path of chaos and still you are all alone.

Ladies, keep your heart, you were built to feel

Passionate and tender, we are not made of steel

Find the courage to love; it's a feeling that heals

Seems like a uphill struggle but you'll find that one who seals the deal

So don't lose your soul along the way,

The key is to love yourself each and every single day.

Oh I get angry, oh I get so angry

Why you gonna let him act this way?

Cut you deep till you feel the pain;

When you gonna stand up, stand to this bully?

He's trying to hold you down, girl you gotta act unruly

See him for what he is, he ain't worthy;

Worthy to be your king, for a king values his queen,

And oh woman you are a queen.

Forget all you have seen in this world full of sin,

For before sin, there was God

And God says you are a queen with a rib of a king.

And a king cares for the woman on his throne,

He works hard and fights for his own;

So he cannot oppress you,

Your story's been told

He cannot repress you,

Woman please be bold.

Find your strength before you become his reflection

Clear your mind from this stupid confusion

Remember who you were born to be

For only then you can truly see that it's time to

Leave this man

Who's not fit to be your king.

BEAUTY OF A BLACK WOMAN

Black woman,

You are more than the roundness of your hips

Or the thickness of your thighs

I know you want to take him on a ride

But first you gotta find

That inner peace that settles your mind

Seek for the beauty within and

Let it shine, let it shine, let it shine

So through you, he will see that illusions

Are just lies

And you don't need to lie to receive acceptance through his eyes

Because you understand why you were created,

A greater power than thine.

Your beauty lies in the strength of your heart

Strong enough to carry him through times that are dark

Your beauty lies in the power of your love

Holding him down when times are rough

Showing him you will be there, that you'll always care

Because you love him past all

The material things that he wears.

So that's where the beauty of a black woman lies

In her strength,

Her integrity and

In a love that never dies.

LOVE YOURSELF

I had to learn to love myself, YES;

First and above everything else

It was the toughest lesson I had to learn

For I was looking for love from everybody else

Needed to fill a hole deep within my soul

The darkest feeling I would ever know

Searched for acceptance through their eyes

Thinking it will be a justification of I

I searched and searched but I didn't find

Instead I dug a deeper hole, made my soul cry.

They had no love to give

The world had sucked them dry

This world's a bitter place,

Humans turn to vultures in order to win the race

But I refused to be broken or resort to their ways.

I realised I had to set a different pace

So I looked to my maker to continue

To bless me with his grace

To love myself regardless of what people say

I will no longer search for acceptance through their eyes

Cos I found acceptance through Jesus Christ

And I'll walk each day by his side

And though, I sometimes fall, he grants me the courage to get back up.

I am a winner, I passed them all.

I would just like to say thank you for following me on this journey of self-discovery, it has not been easy and day by day I am still learning and growing. The world can be sometimes tough, circumstances are thrown at us that we never anticipated and people can be downright cruel but in the midst of it all, we must remember to love ourselves, put ourselves first and do the right thing, It is not always easy to do because we are faced with so many pressures but it is so paramount, so essential because it is the only thing that holds us together. For most of my life, I was looking desperately for someone to love me and the slightest disapproval proved to me that I was unlovable, it happened time and time again that I became convinced that there was nothing to like about me but I was wrong and that's not the way life works; you see anywhere you go in this life someone will always have something negative to say because you cannot please everybody and yes, you do have flaws but who doesn't. Our society is so plagued with the notion of 'perfection' when there is no such thing; Humans are born imperfect and only through God, love and the understanding of these flaws of ourselves and others we are made perfect; yet we seek perfection because we have been repeatedly put down by our fellow others, made to feel like some kind of freak and outsider when the truth is we are all outsiders to a certain degree and we can all learn and grow from each other. For ages, I tried to fit in, I tried to be normal and accepted but I had to learn that I must first accept myself for when someone is truly happy, they do not need another's affirmation; I had to be okay with whom I was, I had to understand my strengths and weaknesses and work on what I could but also understanding that there was nothing wrong with me. The world had to 'take me as I am', if you don't like me, then you can sling it; if you want to criticise and put me down, please find somewhere else to go but if you want to take your time to understand me, I'm good; if you want to teach me another way of seeing things, I'm open, if we need to compromise, that's fine and if we need to disagree to agree then that's fine by me too but I will never let another person make me feel bad about myself again; I have come too far for that. By loving yourself, you prove to the world that you are okay and people will respect and learn from you. We all have something to give, something to share; do not let anyone take that away from you, just live your life the best way you know how and try to do right by others too, that's how I live my life and I can honestly say I'm doing just fine; yes sometimes I struggle like I mentioned earlier about getting depressed or feeling anxious. Some days are good, some are bad but I accept it and start afresh; every second, minute, hour, day is a chance at a fresh start; I take it. Hope you have enjoyed my story, hope it made you smile and I hope you were able to take something out of it.

Forever Living, Forever Loving Life

If the issues in this book has touched or affected you, please contact me on undercurrentspoetry@hotmail.com

Printed in Great Britain
by Amazon

85158144R00058